WHEN I SEND MY CHILD TO CHILD CARE

WHEN I SEND MY CHILD TO CHILD CARE

THE BUSY CAREGIVER'S GUIDE TO HIGH-QUALITY CHILD CARE

MATT TAPSCOTT AND DENISE TAPSCOTT

 iUniverse®

WHEN I SEND MY CHILD TO CHILD CARE
THE BUSY CAREGIVER'S GUIDE TO HIGH-QUALITY CHILD CARE

iUniverse books may be ordered through booksellers or by contacting:

iUniverse
1663 Liberty Drive
Bloomington, IN 47403
www.iuniverse.com
1-800-Authors (1-800-288-4677)

ISBN: 978-1-5320-1318-8 (sc)
ISBN: 978-1-5320-1317-1 (e)

Library of Congress Control Number: 2016921418

Print information available on the last page.

iUniverse rev. date: 09/28/2017

To Samantha, Natalie, and Noah—our awesome children.
Thank you for sharing our home and your lives!

When I Send My Child to Child Care recognizes that all caregivers of young children are busy!

- This easy-to-use guide assists parents and guardians in knowing what to see and discuss in high-quality childcare.
- It is designed to help professional caregivers intentionally deliver essential traits of high-quality childcare.
- For quality childcare to be achieved, the needs of all parties must be addressed.

For forty years the authors have provided childcare and early learning to working families wanting professional childcare services. In our nationally accredited family childcare home and in our roles as administrators or as staff of nationally accredited childcare centers, we have worked with thousands of children and their families in group childcare programs, centers, and homes.

After all these years of service, we continue to be amazed at the absolute magic of children and of early-childhood education as a profession. Unfortunately, we also continue to be amazed at how complicated it can be for families searching for quality childcare and for professional caregivers providing high-quality, best-practice care.

As instructors in our state's Child Care Resource and Referral (CCRR) system teaching best practices to childcare providers and through state, regional, and national workshops and conferences, we have directly instructed hundreds of childcare providers. Through our formal education in early-childhood development, elementary education, and business, we began our careers with a good framework of what young children need developmentally, as well as what operating a childcare business requires professionally.

Through these years of experience and ongoing professional development as childcare providers, we have seen firsthand how children and their caregivers (parents and childcare providers alike) actually utilize childcare environments. Frequently what we have experienced is that what children need, what parents want, and what professional caregivers offer are not connected in a clear understanding of what this critical-need service should look like to all parties involved.

All these experiences helped us create *When I Send My Child to Child Care: The Busy Caregiver's Guide to High-Quality Child Care.* We hope this practical, easy-to-use guide can assist both parents and professional caregivers to better ensure high-quality, best-practice care for children and smooth working relationships between parents and the professional caregivers who deliver these services.

When caring for young children, what matters most is not which of the caregiver roles we fill (parent or professional) but the intentional decisions each caregiver makes about the care provided. Where and how young children (newborn through eight years) spend their childcare days matters greatly. All early-childhood research supports this statement.

Through photographs and concepts, *When I Send My Child to Child Care* is intended to serve as a reference for all busy caregivers.

- Photographs of routine childcare practices like transitions, nutrition, literacy, guidance, caregiver relationships, and other important practices make up this book. The accompanying verse helps you to recognize indicators of quality you should observe routinely in your own childcare setting.

- The adjoining concept page goes into more detail regarding why seeing this particular practice in your childcare program is important.

Eleven million children in the United States attend some form of group childcare every day in a variety of care environments: centers, childcare homes, nannies, kith and kin, relative or close friends, preschools, and so forth. Regardless of where care is provided, there are numerous indicators of quality that need to be observed by the consumer and intentionally implemented by the caregiver to achieve high-quality, best-practice childcare environments.

These observable and intentional practices support the young child's comfortable and developmentally appropriate fit into the routines of group childcare, and they demonstrate a childcare program's effort to achieve research-based standards of high-quality care.

Consumers need to request these high-quality indicators; caregivers need to routinely deliver them. Everyone wins!

When I Send My Child to Child Care asks the primary adult caregivers (parents, for example) to be mindful of the challenges group childcare presents and to the best of your ability send your child ready to participate in the unique dynamic of group childcare. Though it may feel like home to you, it is not, and even if your children can't articulate it, they know it is not. No matter how good their care is, functioning in a group childcare environment is a unique dynamic for everyone involved.

When I Send My Child to Child Care hopes all the caregivers in your children's lives will continue to build healthier relationships with the children and with one another. Though written and photographed with formal childcare settings in mind, these high-quality concepts can be applied in most childcare environments—formal and informal.

Here is how this book is arranged:

The photo page of each section is told in a playful rhyme as a child might experience it in high-quality child care.

The concept page is opposite the photo page and details the importance of that section's quality indicator.

Caregiver conversations suggest ideas for communication between adult caregivers. Several of these conversations include an author's note and approaches we have taken in similar situations.

Quality indicator checklist: At the back of the book and corresponding to each section is a two-page, nineteen-point checklist.

Journal pages: At the very end of the book are journal pages where you may record conversations, ideas, and your family's personal experiences in childcare.

Are the concepts in this book part of your child's routine childcare program? If so, thank your caregivers and support them in their wonderful work. If not, how can you support your caregivers in implementing more indicators of quality in your childcare program? Caregiver conversations, for example.

Sections

Prepared for Group Child Care: "I need to have my family's love before my childcare day."

Transitions: "When I go to childcare, my caregiver greets me by name."

Ratios: "They keep us safer as we learn and play."

Handwashing: "We wash our hands throughout the day."

Nutrition: "The meal they serve is serving to build my brain."

Reading: "The words I hear, the pictures I see, the things we talk about."

Free Play: "In space safe and fun"

Self-Selection: "It's a wonderful way to teach!"

Guidance: "They help us learn and talk about the feelings that we have."

Outside: "The value of nature in our lives"

Rest Time: "A story read, a blanket spread, we lie upon our mats."

Screen Time: "Our caregiver knows active play is what helps us thrive"

My Caregiver Is a Professional: "They attend professional development classes."

The Cost of High-Quality Child Care: "The incredible cost to everyone is nearly impossible to bear!"

It Takes a Village: "Knowing when we work together"

From the Caregivers Who Experienced This Book: "We continue to be amazed at the absolute magic of children—and of early childhood as a profession."

Resource Page: We Are Not Alone

Quality Indicator Checklist: Before we make our childcare choice

Journal Pages: Observations and experiences in childcare

I need to have my family's love before my childcare day.
It makes a tremendous difference in how I learn, act, and play!
Some downtime at home, a good night's rest, and some healthy food—
all these are important in setting my childcare mood.

Prepared for Group Child Care

Love requires all caregivers in a child's life to make good and sometimes difficult decisions.

All children, but particularly young children who attend group childcare environments, need downtime when they are not required to negotiate multiple relationships, various rules, personalities, and environments. Few children can be on the go all the time and be successfully well behaved in every environment, especially a group childcare environment full of young children.

Helping to provide enough structure and consistency for the developing child while also providing enough flexibility and independence to the child as he or she grows takes practice and time. Be patient and understanding. Love is a balance and often a challenging balance as children grow. Children who attend group childcare need regular opportunities to relax and play outside of this special dynamic.

Caregiver Conversations

- How will we, the adult caregivers of this child, communicate when things are going well and if they are not? Face-to-face, in writing, on the phone?
- What do you expect of me/us, the child's parent(s) or guardian(s)?
- What do you expect of me/us, the professional caregiver(s)?
- What does "a good fit" mean to each of us? (See the "It Takes a Village" section.)

When I go to childcare, my caregiver greets me by name.
"Good morning, [child's name]. I am so happy that you came."
I have a little cubby; it belongs just to me.
I keep my special things there for my parents to see.

Transitions

Going from the child's home to the daylong care of another person can be a difficult transition for young children and for parents as well. We are asking a lot of everyone in this transition—including the professional caregiver.

When the professional caregiver is physically and mentally prepared and the environment is ready for children to arrive, including a special space for their personal items, transitions go better. When the child and the parent or guardian are warmly and genuinely welcomed by name and the professional caregiver knows the child's interests and temperament, transitions go better.

When the child arrives at childcare after a good night's rest, some quality time with family, and well nourished, transitions go better.

When parents are confident that childcare arrangements are the best possible choice for their child, transitions go better.

When transitions go better, childcare goes better.

In best-practice childcare environments, children will have some type of a transitional area for personal things. This provides a sense of belonging for the child; it says, "I have space here just for me!" Additionally, this space provides transitional space for children and the parent/guardian to say to one another, "I will see you after work/school. Have a wonderful day. I love you!" as the parent/guardian transitions the child into the care of the professional childcare provider.

Note: Parents and Guardians, never sneak out of childcare when you think your child is not looking. Doing so makes transitions harder in the long run. When your child realizes you have left without having said good-bye, this can be very upsetting. They may fear that people who love them can just be gone. This often makes for a much more difficult transition for the child and the caregiver. It is always best to be honest in your transition as you, your child, and the caregiver begin your days by saying, "Good-bye. I will see you after work/school."

Caregiver Conversations

- Where will my child store their personal items (clothing, shoes, etc.) while in your care?
- How do you handle a child wanting to use something out of his or her personal storage space (a toy or blanket, for example) during the day if the child can do so without it causing too many program problems?

My caregiver cares genuinely for me,
my friends, our play space, and all our needs.
Ratios equal the right number of children each day;
they keep us safer as we learn and play!

Ratios

Ratios in childcare refer to the number of children for every caregiver in the program. Ratios matter greatly.

Many states have ratio guidelines, rules, or licensing standards regarding the number of children a caregiver can care for. In addition, most states have square footage or space requirements for each child in the program. Most ratio guidelines are often a minimum requirement and not necessarily best-practice standards. Currently, there is no national ratio standard.

Ratios are very important and need to be strongly considered when choosing childcare environments. For example, a ratio of 1:6 is one experienced, knowledgeable, adult caregiver caring for six children. This may seem like a lot of children, but to a well-organized, rested-and-ready, professional caregiver this number works. Additionally, the number of very young children (generally newborns to eighteen months) in a care environment needs to be considered. The National Association for the Education of Yong Children (NAEYC) recommends a ratio of no more than 1:3 for infants and toddlers (newborn through twenty-four months). Infants and young toddlers require more time and attention. Ratios matter.

Seem simple enough? That's not always the case in childcare. In order to make it financially, some childcare programs will care for more children than is best practice for the children or the caregiver. Some providers will set their childcare rates according to what they feel the families they serve can afford and make up the difference by adding more children in their care. This may seem well intentioned, but children ultimately pay the price when there are too many children, not enough space, and too few caregivers (or caregivers who are simply exhausted). Children may be safe, but too little of what children actually need, such as nurturing, one-on-one time, and engaged adults assisting children as necessary in group care, can be achieved with ratios out of balance.

Caregiver Conversations

- What is the highest number of children you will care for at any one time?
- What recognized ratio guidelines do you follow regarding the number of children you care for each day? For example: NAEYC. (See the Resource page.)
- Authors' note: "It is the way we have always done it" is an unacceptable response in relation to a caregiver caring for too many children. We suggest you consider other childcare arrangements if confronted with this situation.

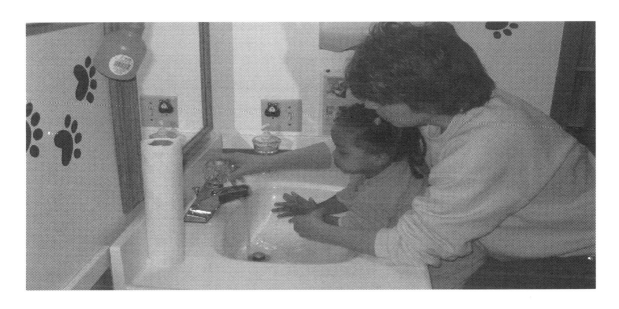

We wash our hands throughout the day using water, soap, and towels.
We wash them while we sing ABCs—all the consonants and vowels.

Handwashing

Handwashing has been recognized by the National Institute of Health as an important way to manage the spread of infectious diseases in childcare centers. At test centers, handwashing helped reduce colds when frequent and proper handwashing practices were incorporated into the program.

In group childcare, handwashing can be a daunting, time-consuming, and fairly expensive (paper towels, soap, etc.) process. However, there is no excuse for not having a process of frequent handwashing with young children. There is no better way of reducing the spread of infectious diseases in childcare programs.

For children and caregivers in any group childcare environment, handwashing must be a common practice occurring several times every day.

According to the Center for Disease Control (CDC) here is the preferred five-step handwashing method:

1. Wet your hands with clean, running water (warm or cold), turn off the tap, and apply soap.
2. Lather your hands by rubbing them together with the soap. Be sure to lather the backs of your hands, between your fingers, and under your nails.
3. Scrub your hands for at least twenty seconds. Need a timer? Sing the ABC song from beginning to end.
4. Rinse your hands well under clean running water.
5. Dry your hands using a clean towel, or air-dry them.

Caregiver Conversations

- Talk about several different times throughout each day when handwashing occurs in childcare.
    - o   Upon arrival
    - o   Before and after sensory play activities
    - o   Before and after snacks and meals
    - o   After toileting and diapering
- What is your process for regularly cleaning and sanitizing childcare equipment and play materials?

We always have a balanced meal that includes protein, dairy, fruit, and grains.
My caregiver knows the meal they serve is serving to build my brain!

Nutrition

The food children are provided during the first few years of life is necessary for healthy body and brain growth. Team Nutrition, a child nutrition program at the US Department of Agriculture, suggests the reason we eat is to fuel our bodies for the activities we do. This is particularly important for developing children.

Childcare provides an early-in-life opportunity for a caregiver, who is not the parent, to model excellent nutrition choices. Choosing fresh food first (as possible), then frozen, then canned is an easy procedure to remember: fresh, frozen, canned. Creating menus high in grains, fruits, and vegetables; quality proteins (including beans and legumes); and a variety of dairy items ensures children are getting the fuel their bodies require. And without question, limit sweets and overly processed foods. All these intentional food choices help ensure children are being exposed to and choosing the quality fuel their bodies require for optimum growth and development.

One indicator of an excellent, high-quality childcare program is the family-style meal. These meals are served at the table in individual serving bowls supporting children in serving themselves with assistance as necessary. Nutrition research shows that children experiencing family-style meals learn to make better food choices, develop self-help skills, and have advanced language skills. Family-style meals take practice and intention, and the caregiver must be well prepared for this activity.

Do you have difficult eaters? A practice the authors have successfully used for more than twenty-five years is the two-job concept. The caregiver has the first job: to prepare and serve a balanced, nutritious meal. The children have the second job: to choose from the balanced meal presented what they will eat. This approach may present a significant change in thinking for many adults. Letting children choose? But think for a moment how straightforward this approach is. As the adult caregiver, if you have done your job by providing a balanced, nutritious meal, let the children do their job—choose! Following the two-job concept helps eliminate considerable stress around meals, and over time children generally become more accepting of a wider variety of foods. Try hard to not argue with your young child about meals and eating. Rarely does it result in the outcome we are trying to achieve—quality family mealtime.

Caregiver Conversations

- Discuss with your caregiver nutritious menus, family-style meals, and the two-job concept.
- What often helps mealtime to work in group childcare when new foods are introduced is the attitude of the caregiver and the willingness of at least one other child to try the new food. Another strategy is to pair new food with existing favorites.
- The caregiver's willingness and attitude about mealtimes are observable practices that help set the mood for a more relaxed snack or mealtime.
- Authors' note: Group childcare is a unique dynamic. Getting one child to eat a variety of foods can be a challenge. Serving a family-style, balanced meal to multiple children who bring a wide variety of eating experiences requires a great deal of effort, practice, and patience.

Every day there is reading—at least twenty minutes per day.
My caregiver knows books are important in many, many ways.
The words I hear, the pictures I see, the things we talk about;
I can learn so very much with a variety of books about.

Reading

Reading is magical!

Studies show that children who are read to early in their lives are more likely to become strong readers themselves. Reading is a key to school success. This is as certain as the sun rising.

Adults who talk with infants, toddlers, and preschoolers about the books they read and the songs they sing together help children develop language skills. This builds the foundation for later reading skills.

Age-appropriate books (including infant and young toddler board books) allow for children to learn how to hold the book, turn the pages, point to pictures they recognize, and name items. These are important pre-reading skills and need to be presented beginning at birth to help set children on the path to a lifetime of reading enjoyment.

Even school-age children enjoy reading out loud, and it's a great opportunity to bond over a shared book experience.

Caregiver Conversations

- Are there opportunities for children to read independently by touching, looking at, and generally exploring books?
- Is there age-appropriate group time for reading, as well as one-on-one reading when possible?
- Are there age-appropriate books? Are there nonfiction books, as well as fiction books? Does it appear literacy is important in this caregiver's program?
- Authors' note: Observe the childcare environment. How many books are present? How are they displayed? Are books available for children to self-select?
- The authors' practice has always been to help children in our care learn that "books are special; books are not toys," and replacement is expensive. All caregivers need to help their children learn to use and respect books from the children's earliest introduction to them.

There is always time for free play in space safe and fun.
It meets the needs of all my friends—both the big and little ones!

Free Play

Free play as a learning tool is invaluable for young children as they move about the childcare environment (play space), intentionally adding new materials to their often complex play. Free play is not anything goes, although to the untrained eye it may look like organized chaos. Quality free play is intentional and organized to support the individual play styles of each child.

The quality caregiver knows that in children's complex play they are creating, counting, problem solving, communicating, negotiating, compromising, and building confidence. These are all skills necessary for healthy success as children grow and participate in the bigger world around them. During free play in quality childcare, children are encouraged to make choices and incorporate new items into this creative style of learning. The authors believe these are the preschool skills children need to succeed and are fully achieved in a quality play-based learning environment.

The caregiver may be engaged by being supportive or by role-playing with the children, but they should not constantly be in charge of or directing the play. The caregiver is responsible for overall supervision and assistance as needed, but the environmental setup (how the childcare space is organized) supports children in exploring and expanding their play.

Regardless of the childcare environment selected, supervision by knowledgeable and experienced caregivers is fundamental. Engaged caregivers aware of the children and their particular play styles is a key to success in any quality care environment.

Caregiver Conversations

- Discuss play as learning. What does the phrase "play is the work of early childhood" mean to each of you? Play space intentionally arranged to allow children to make independent play choices helps children make better choices routinely. Well-designed play spaces often reduce challenging behaviors.
- What is the normal routine of the day in childcare? Is it set in stone, or is it flexible yet consistent to meet children's various and changing needs and interests?
- Be clear with one another about supervision of the children. Will my child ever be left unsupervised? Define clearly what supervision means to each of you.
- Authors' note: Child caring space intentionally and safely arranged for children allows for creative and safe play. Caregivers may themselves be using the bathroom, checking on lunch, or assisting another child and not be in the same space as your child 100 percent of the time. This type of caregiving is a more common practice in childcare homes than centers. Parents need to know and discuss this with the caregiver in advance. Observe when you visit how free play and supervision is working in the program you are considering.

There is a wide variety of toys on shelves that I can reach.
When I can self-select the toys I like,
it's a wonderful way to teach!

Self-Selection

The child caring environment should have toys situated in such a way that children are able to self-select many of the things that interest them. Additionally, there must be enough toys and equipment to meet the needs relative to the group size and the various ages of the children.

Incredible learning occurs when children can self-select toys and materials. Children learn to make good choices, take turns, and become more creative in their play and problem solving as they add to and adapt their play. When the childcare space is arranged so children can self-select, children build confidence in their decision making. Caregivers who have toys readily accessible and of sufficient number for the children in care is demonstrating that they are tuned in to the interests and play styles of each child.

Children who must wait for the caregiver to make toy selections available are often frustrated children. For example, if I have to ask for many of the toys/materials I need, the natural ebb and flow of my play and learning is constantly interrupted. Self-selection arrangement of materials eliminates a great deal of this frustration for children and demonstrates that the caregiver is supporting how children play and learn.

Another quality indicator is cleanup. Caregivers help children develop, through lots of practice, a cleanup routine. The caregiver might say, "In two minutes we are going to start cleanup so we can have lunch." In two minutes they begin singing the "cleanup, cleanup, everybody, everywhere" song, for example. Direction is given to those who need it, assistance is given to those who need it, and those too young to participate may be the caregiver's helpers, staying close to the caregiver and placing a toy back on a shelf or into a wash bucket to be cleaned. It was a group effort to play; it should be a group effort to clean.

Caregiver Conversations

- Discuss child-centered learning, the environment (childcare space), and self-selection of materials.
- Ask: Is there space in the environment (in either the center or home) that is off-limits to children? How are children helped to understand this limit?
- Is there a sufficient number of toys and materials available compared to the number of children in care?
- How does the caregiver help children participate in cleanup?
- Discuss sharing. Taking turns is often what well-intentioned adults mean when they "make children share," even though the child may not be finished using the toy, materials, or equipment in question. Children who are allowed to decide when they are done using something are children who learn to share best. Children who are forced to share before they actually understand the concept learn that no piece of equipment is ever safe from being taken away—no matter how engaged they are in its use. That is frustrating!

It's not always easy with a large group of friends!
Sometimes someone gets sad or even mad and things get out of hand.
But my caregiver knows and understands that none of us are bad.
They help us learn and talk about the feelings that we have.

Guidance

Children cannot learn to be good by being made to feel bad.

The goal of guidance is for children to learn as they grow to regulate their own behavior toward acceptable social interactions and problem solving. The authors believe this is the very essence of being good—for both children and adults.

Adult caregivers must have both patience and understanding in guiding young children in group childcare.

- Patience: knowing each child in the group brings numerous and varied life experiences.
- Understanding: knowledge that every child is in a different place in their chronological and emotional development.

Discipline should not be administered as punishment, because guidance toward self-regulation is the ultimate goal. Be patient and understand that children learn through repeated experiences—repeated and repeated and repeated! Just because a one-, two-, three-, or four-year-old (or older) can be good in many situations doesn't mean that child can be good in *every* situation. Having both patience and understanding takes time and practice for all caregivers. Guidance, like children's growth, is a process.

Caregiver Conversations

- Discuss each caregiver's (parent and professional) understanding of guidance versus punishment.
- Discuss how a child-centered environment reduces challenging behaviors.
- Discuss each caregiver's perspective on the idea that patience is one thing, and understanding age-appropriate development is another. Talk about this.
- My caregiver will not use physical or emotional punishment as a discipline technique.
- Use the journal pages in the back of this book to record your ideas, thoughts, and even your frustrations! All caregivers have them at some point.

Getting dressed to go outside can take a lot of time,
but our caregiver knows the value of nature in our lives!

Outside

The curriculum that nature provides is impossible to duplicate. Nature is a most incredible teacher!

No matter the child's age or experience, nature (even a small green space in your own backyard or a potted plant on a patio) welcomes each child with open arms. Nature is perfectly equipped to allow each child to learn at his or her own pace. Studies show that children who routinely experience natural environments firsthand learn to respect the earth and grow up knowing better how to care for and protect this valuable resource—our planet.

Children who spend long hours in group childcare need to be outside on a very regular basis. Daily is the ideal.

Caregiver Conversations

- How often do the children go outside? Are you always with them outdoors?
- Is there adequate outdoor play space for the number of children in your care?
- Does the outdoor space lend itself to safe, self-exploration (with appropriate supervision)?
- Do you leave the childcare premises for walks or field trips? May other adult caregivers (parents, for example) join you on these outings?
- Who is responsible for ensuring children have what they need for outside play—for example, boots, coats, hats, mittens, and so forth, for cold-weather play or changes of clothing for water and messy play? Is sunscreen or bug repellent applied? Who provides these items? Is parental permission obtained for applying it? Doing so is a best practice.
- Authors note: The lack of a playground structure does not mean a program is missing something. Nature-based play is intentionally very open and allows children to explore the environment in more creative ways. Observe. How are children currently using the outside play space when nature-based play is the focus?

We play, we learn, we eat our lunch, and then we get ready for our naps.
A story read, a blanket spread, we lie upon our mats.
Maybe one hour or maybe two—it depends upon our age.
My caregiver knows that "on demand" is an appropriate infant stage.

Rest Time

There are numerous unique demands on everyone in childcare environments, and everyone needs a break during the day—caregivers, as well as children. In programs that focus on children's social, emotional, and physical needs, most children are ready for and in need of some rest time after several hours of creative play and learning.

Caregivers (at both homes and centers) should have some formal policy/plan about rest time for all the children in their program, including older children. Although older children may have outgrown their need for a nap, many caregivers have the need in a typical full day for some type of break. Everyone in the program benefits from some routine downtime even if that time is an organized, quiet activity.

Infants should rest on-demand. Newborns and infants cannot wait for quiet time, so the concept of on-demand is an appropriate stage of development. This means the caregiver assists the child to sleep when the child needs to sleep, as well as eat when the child needs to eat. A knowledgeable caregiver recognizes when a child is saying through their words and actions that he or she needs a break, some food, or a diaper change. The caregiver does not let the program schedule or routine determine the care for newborns and infants but rather the child's needs. On-demand develops young children's ability to ask for a break and learn through this experience that the world is a safe and predictable place.

Caregiver Conversations

- Where do children nap?
- Do they have their own sleeping items—mats, blankets, and the like?
- How often are these items laundered if provided by the caregiver?
- What do you know about on-demand needs, and how will you use that knowledge for my infant?
- Is there space for on-demand napping while other children are still actively playing?
- Discuss the safe-sleep method for infants.
- Talk about older children who have outgrown naps. How do you help them take a break? How long is this break period? How can I, as the child's parent/guardian, help this time be most successful for you and for my child?

Our caregiver knows active play is what helps us thrive,
but recognizes that media is also part of our lives.
So if we do use television, or screens of any kind,
the caregiver ensures its quality and daily 2 hours or less (home and care) combined.

Screen Time

Television and screen time in general, regardless of the content, should be used sparingly and intentionally, particularly for young children in group childcare environments. Young children learn best by interacting with people.

According to the American Academy of Pediatrics, television and other entertainment media should be avoided for infants and children younger than two. A child's brain develops rapidly during the first five years, and it is important for children to spend time experiencing outdoor play, using books, and using their imagination in free play. Children should not be sitting in front of a television or computer for hours on end. When the decision is made to use television in early-learning programs, PBSKIDS is a respected, quality choice. PBSKIDS is committed to age-appropriate early learning with an emphasis on science, technology, engineering, and math (STEM). The very best practice, when using screen time in a childcare program, recommends the caregiver participate with children in their media viewing. This allows for engagement, and screen time becomes less passive.

Older children and teens should engage with entertainment media for no more than one or two hours per day, and that should also be of high-quality content.

Caregiver Conversations

- Discuss the use of screen time in your child's day, both at home and in child care.
- What television, computer or gaming programs do you allow the children in your care to use?
- Is my child required to participate in this activity, or are they allowed to make other activity choices during that time?

My caregiver is a professional, it is evident to see.
They attend professional development classes;
it helps them better care for me!

My Caregiver Is a Professional

Professional caregivers (often referred to as providers or teachers) realize the importance of participating in ongoing professional development. This supports the caregiver keeping current with research in early childhood brain development, as well as changing strategies in childcare and early learning. It is also valuable for caregivers to connect with a network of other professional caregivers.

Ongoing professional development is a significant commitment of time professional caregivers make on top of the actual work of caring for a group of children. This is noteworthy. Most ongoing professional development for childcare occurs after hours (evenings and weekends) when children are not being cared for in the group care program. This makes for a very long workweek for caregivers who are already, as a rule, generally underpaid. Childcare programs that offer odd-hour care (overnight care, for example) have an entirely different and challenging schedule they must figure out in order to attend professional development.

Additionally, most states have minimum requirements for professional development hours for regulated childcare providers, as well as the content of the training a caregiver must achieve annually. You can research what these requirements are in your state through your state's Department of Family Services or Department of Human Services, generally the department responsible for your state's childcare system.

Note: Professional development does make for a long workweek for your caregiver, but in the field of professional childcare services, like any other profession, it is what professionals do. Ongoing professional development matters.

Caregiver Conversations

- What ongoing professional development plan do you have in place?
- What do you do, unrelated to your work as a caregiver, to take care of you—hobbies and interests, for example?

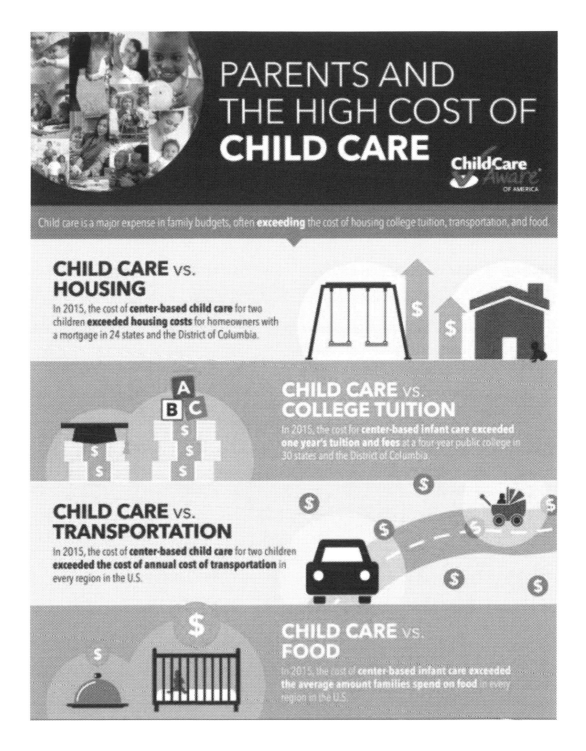

Working families require this "critical-need service" called childcare.
But the incredible cost to everyone is nearly impossible to bear!
Creative plans and tax incentives, a broader conversation there must be.
The current childcare funding system is not working well for me!

The Cost of High-Quality Child Care

Childcare is expensive, both for parents purchasing the service and for the professionals delivering this service.

- Next to mortgages and rent, childcare is often one of the largest out-of-pocket expenses for most working families in the United States.
- For the childcare program, reinvesting their small profit margin back into the business, the cost is also high: staff, rent/mortgage, utilities, food, toys, equipment, and so on. And yet the average caregiver makes less than $20,000 a year, and they often work with few employment benefits available.
- Nearly 75 percent of American families are in the workforce requiring childcare services. Childcare is a critical-need service.

Ensuring the quality of and access to this critical-need service is a good investment. For every dollar invested in high-quality childcare research shows the investment pays seven to ten times in dividends. Children cared for well early in life are more successful later in life. It's pretty simple, actually.

However, providing high-quality childcare presents a unique business model. To ensure quality, adult-to-child staffing ratios must be maintained, but doing so imposes a restricted profit margin on the program.

The problem is evident: There are not enough state and federal investments in childcare compared to the large percentage of working families requiring these critical need services. Private efforts alone cannot meet the need. Too many consumers piece together their childcare options, which is frustrating for parents needing service, workers delivering service, and, most importantly, our children, who literally get caught in the middle. Caregivers can't just raise their rates as is sometimes suggested; working families are already struggling with the high cost of quality childcare.

There are no caregiver conversations attached to this section, and there are no easy answers for this conversation. There are creative ideas, such as significantly increased tax incentives for professionals providing this critical-need service. The authors believe societal and political investments are required to vastly improve our national childcare system. This system, as it has long operated, falls far short of meeting the needs of children, parents, and professional caregivers. Society and our economy pay a big price for this. New, creative sources of support must become a national priority.

All the caregivers in my life, they know without a doubt,
the more they share about my care the better it turns out!
They talk about me growing and all my wonderful needs;
knowing when we work together—they trust I will succeed!

It Takes a Village

Caring for children professionally in group childcare requires a unique effort and a special relationship between the primary caregivers (parent, foster parent, etc.) and secondary caregivers (professional childcare providers), as well as any other caring adults responsible for the child. Achieving the best possible balance, considerate of everyone's needs, requires a relationship of communication and trust developed through diligence and over time.

You can help your child and their caregiver connect each day by talking with the caregiver about the time your child was not in their care:

- Tell your caregiver whether your child had a normal night or a busy or out-of-the-norm night—sleepless, fussy, and the like.
- What has your child eaten before coming to childcare?
- The provider, knowing how your child is feeling that day, can better organize the childcare day for everyone in the group.

Respect the policies and procedures of the program you have chosen:

- Adhere to drop-off and pickup times; don't change the caregiver's work schedule without notice.
- Strictly follow the childcare fee payment schedule; after all, this is the professional caregiver's paycheck.
- Respect wellness policies. A wellness policy generally means the child is not only healthy but also rested and ready to participate in a group childcare environment. Being sick is not the only reason a child should not be in childcare.
- Ask for regular conferences (at least annually) to be sure you, the professional caregiver, and your child are all still doing well together in this program.

Adherence to policies is no small matter to your child's professional caregivers. It shows you understand how hard they work in providing a high-quality program to a group of young children each and every day. Adherence to program policies allows the caregiver to focus on the most important aspect of their work, the children.

What can you expect from your child's professional caregiver?

Without question, you should expect safe care. You need to expect that your caregiver is keenly aware of the incredible growth your child is experiencing during these first and crucial years of life. Therefore, the caregivers need to intentionally create safe, age-appropriate, play-based care and early-learning environments for your child and for the entire group of children in their care. Group childcare is a unique dynamic. It is, at times, a tricky balance and requires an intentional, sustained effort. When you see this effort occurring in your child's care program, let your caregivers know that you appreciate it. Professional caregivers appreciate their efforts being recognized by the families they serve. Developing an open line of communication is a key to success in your childcare arrangements.

From the Caregivers Who Experienced This Book

For forty years we have worked in the field of early childhood education, and we continue to be amazed at the absolute magic of children and of early childhood education as a profession. Unfortunately, we also continue to be amazed at how complicated it can be for families searching for quality childcare and for the professional caregiver providing best-practice care.

We hope this easy-to-use guide will reduce some frustrations in what to look for and how to ensure, to the best of your ability, that your child is attending a high-quality, best-practice, childcare environment.

Throughout our careers in childcare and early learning, we (along with our three awesome children) have shared our professional lives and often our home caring for hundreds of children in various group childcare environments. Through years of hands-on experience, education, and best-practice research, we recognize quality childcare and early learning are one in the same. We believe anyone who attempts to separate the two (childcare and early learning) is doing a disservice to children and is not being forthright with parents.

Professionally, we have done the following:

- provided childcare in childcare centers of various sizes and in a nationally accredited child development home caring for newborns through school-age children
- served children whose families have the economic resources available for a very comfortable lifestyle and children whose families struggle economically to provide for basic needs
- taught childcare business classes to providers; presented workshops at state, regional, and national childcare conferences; and continue to advocate politically for improvements to our childcare delivery system
- helped organize Iowa childcare home providers into Iowa's first childcare union, so this community of professionals caring for children through in-home care is a tradition maintained and enriched
- active members of state and national childcare professional associations

With numerous quality rating and improvement systems (QRIS) occurring in many states throughout our country, what we still see missing in childcare is a practical, easy-to-use guide connecting the busy adult caregivers (both parents and professional caregivers) on the same page. We hope we have achieved some of this connection in the pages of *When I Send My Child to Child Care*.

Enjoy this book and early childhood. It is an amazing time!
Matt and Denise Tapscott
Continue the conversation with us on Facebook at Almost Home early learning - naturally

Resource Page: We Are Not Alone

US Department of Agriculture; Child and Adult Care Food Program (CACFP)
http://www.fns.usda.gov/tn/team-nutrition

National Institutes of Health (NIH)
www.ncbi.nlm.nih.gov/pubmed/9052131

Safe Sleep Practices
http://www.cdc.gov/sids/Parents-Caregivers.htm

Center for Disease Control (CDC)
http://www.cdc.gov/handwashing

PBSKIDS.org
http://pbskids.org/

Center for Childcare Workforce (CCW)
http://www.aft.org/node

Economic Policy Institute (EPI): It's time for an ambitious national investment in America's children
http://www.epi.org/publication/its-time-for-an-ambitious-national-investment-in-americas-children/

Child Care Aware
http://childcareaware.org/

National Association for Family Child Care (NAFCC)
http://www.nafcc.org/

National Association for the Education of Young Children (NAEYC)
http://www.naeyc.org/

American Academy of Pediatrics (AAP)
http://pediatrics.aappublications.org

Quality Indicator Checklist

These indicators help identify that your childcare program is delivering recognized high-quality care. The resource page can assist you with more details when using this checklist.

1. _____ **Prepared for group childcare:** My child has had a good night's rest and a nutritious meal before I take him or her to childcare. Yes! The first responsibility of a good childcare experience falls to you, the parent, as the primary caregiver.

2. _____ **Transitions:** My caregiver greets me and my child by name upon arrival and assists my child's transition from our home into the childcare environment.

3. _____ **Ratios:** I am aware of the number of children cared for in my childcare program. It meets recognized ratio guidelines of my state's Department of Family Services or Department of Human Services.

4. _____ **Handwashing:** I have talked with my caregiver about the importance and frequency of handwashing.
   _____ We practice this in our home as well.

5. _____ **Nutrition:** I talk with my caregiver routinely about the nutritious meals and snacks we serve to my child while in childcare as well as in our own home and how important nutrition is to my child's healthy development.

6. _____ **Reading:** Age-appropriate children's books are available and displayed in the child-caring space.
   _____ The caregiver routinely shares with me some of the books read with my child or to the group of children.

7. _____ **Free play:** We have discussed, and I am comfortable with, the normal routine/ schedule of the childcare day my child will be taking part in.

8. _____ **Self-selection:** The environment (play space and living space) in which my child will be cared for has adequate equipment, toys, and age-appropriate materials, as well as soft or quiet space for alone time as needed.

9. _____ **Play-based learning:** Both my caregiver and I support play as an important part of children learning.

10. _____ **Guidance:** We have discussed the difference between guidance and discipline.
    _____ My caregiver will not use physical or emotional punishment as a discipline technique.

11. _____ **Outside:** I know the caregivers philosophy about children being outdoors. I have observed children in this program playing outside.
    _____ The outside play area is safe and free of debris, such as animal feces.

12. _____ **Rest time:** My caregiver has a policy/plan about rest time for all children in the program, including older school-age children.
    _____ We have discussed on-demand scheduling for infants and their need to sleep on a different schedule from older children's.
    _____ We have discussed safe-sleep practices for infants. (See the resources page for information regarding safe sleep.)

13. _____ **Screen time:** Screen time use has been discussed. Children do not use media as a significant part of their routine childcare day, and when screen time is used, it is child-appropriate programming (PBSKIDS, for example).

14. _____ **My caregiver is a professional:** My caregiver has a professional development plan and shares his or her ongoing professional accomplishments with me.

15. _____ **The cost of care:** We have discussed and settled on childcare fees and a payment schedule.

    _____ We have discussed some factors impacting childcare costs and how childcare programs provide a critical-need service to the community and require additional community advocacy and support.

16. _____ **It takes a village:** My caregiver and I have discussed the role each of us plays in ensuring a good childcare fit. I understand my responsibility as the child's parent ("Prepared for Group Child Care") and the role the caregiver plays in ensuring a safe, family-friendly, child-centered program ("My Caregiver Is a Professional").

    _____ The caregiver and I have discussed, agreed on, and signed written childcare policies.

17. _____ **Resources page:** I have explored at least two professional sites noted on the We Are Not Alone page.

18. _____ **Checklist.** I have completed this checklist before making my childcare choice.

19. _____ **Journal.** I have recorded at least one idea or experience on a journal page.

Journal

(Notes: observations of care, experiences in care, or drawings.)
Suggestion: Date your entries.

Journal

(Notes: observations of care, experiences in care, or drawings.)
Suggestion: Date your entries.

Journal
(Notes: observations of care, experiences in care, or drawings.)
Suggestion: Date your entries.

Journal
(Notes: observations of care, experiences in care, or drawings.)
Suggestion: Date your entries.

Wondering what you need to see in high-quality childcare?

When I Send My Child to Child Care recognizes that all caregivers of young children are busy.

- This practical guide assists parents and guardians in knowing what to look for and discuss in high-quality childcare.
- It is designed to also help professional caregivers intentionally deliver essential indicators of high-quality childcare.
- For the very best quality to be achieved, the needs of all parties must be met.

In this easy-to-use guide, you will find the following:

1. Photo pages showing childcare routines such as transitions, meals, handwashing, play, guidance, and more
2. Concept pages to understand why seeing each of these routines in practice is important
3. Caregiver conversations to assist in achieving high-quality childcare that benefits all parties involved
4. Quality indicator checklists to help make or assess your current childcare decision
5. Resource page: You Are Not Alone, which lists helpful websites

As professional caregivers for forty years, Matt and Denise Tapscott, share real-life examples of best-practice, high-quality childcare indicators and how these benefit children, parents, and the professional caregivers. It takes a village!

When I Send My Child to Child Care

Printed in the United States
By Bookmasters